CHOPIN

PRELUDES FOR THE PIANO

MW01148530

EDITED BY WILLARD A. PALMER

AN ALFRED MASTERWORK EDITION

Cover art: *A detail from* Pont Neuf, Paris
by Pierre-Auguste Renoir (French, 1841–1919)
© 1992 National Gallery of Art, Washington

Book Alone
ISBN-10: 0-7390-0441-7
ISBN-13: 978-0-7390-0441-8

Book & CD
ISBN-10: 0-7390-4754-X
ISBN-13: 978-0-7390-4754-5

Autograph of the Prelude in C Major, Opus 28, No.1

PRELUDES

THE PRELUDES OF FREDERIC CHOPIN
Opus 28

Chopin did not regard himself as a romantic composer. He is said to have disliked the word "romanticism." At the time these preludes were written they were considered revolutionary. Even today several of them (for example, the A Minor Prelude) sound somewhat atonal. Today Chopin's music is regarded as the quintessence of romanticism, and the Preludes are considered by many to be Chopin's most masterful works. The circumstances under which they were composed are abundant in romantic overtones and legends.

When Chopin moved from Palma, on the Balearic island of Majorca, to the monastery at Valdemosa, he was overcome with the beauty of the setting. On December 14, 1838, he had written to his friend Julian Fontana, "Tomorrow I go to that wonderful monastery of Valdemosa, to compose in the cell of some old monk who perhaps had more fire in his soul than I have . . . I think I will soon send you

my preludes and the ballade." Later he wrote of "this sky, the poetry that breathes in everything here, the color of this marvelous place, which human eyes have not yet erased."

But the winter brought violent weather to Majorca. Pouring rains, bitter cold, heavy snowfalls, dense fogs. It was difficult for Chopin to get the proper food, and he became very ill. His principal undertaking at Valdemosa was to complete his 24 preludes, one in each major and minor key, very probably inspired by the *Well-Tempered Clavier* of J. S. Bach. He wrote that he was working at "an old untouchable square writing desk I can scarcely use. On it is a leaden candlestick (a great luxury here) with a candle. Music of Bach, my own scribblings, old papers (not mine) and silence. One can shout — still silence."

The tales surrounding the completion of the Preludes, related by George Sand in her book *Un hiver en Majorque* (A Winter in Majorca), have been discounted by many modern biographers. She tells of an old, demented monastery servant who toured the corridors of the monastery each night, knocking at the cell doors with a shepherd's staff, calling the names of long-dead monks. At Chopin's door he called "Nicolas! Nicolas!" (the name of Chopin's dead father). She tells of black-robed figures with horns and beaks parading in the fog, later discovered to be peasants participating in a carnival masquerade. She relates how Chopin played one prelude in a trance, imagining himself to be dead as he await-ed the arrival of George Sand and her son one night when  they were delayed in returning from Palma because of a pouring rainstorm. As they entered the monastery, drenched and exhausted, Chopin jumped up from the piano bench with a dazed expression. "Ah," he exclaimed, "I knew you were no longer alive!"

Whether such stories are true or untrue, one must remember that George Sand *was* with Chopin, and her accounts must be accepted as the most reliable ones at our disposal. She certainly did succeed in attaching to the 15th Prelude the title "Raindrop Prelude," over Chopin's explicit objections.

Chopin died, calling the name of George Sand, on the morning of October 17, 1849. Three of his compositions were played at the funeral. They were the Preludes in E Minor and B Minor and the Funeral March from the Sonata in Bb Minor.

ORIGIN

Chopin's *PRELUDES*, Opus 28, were completed at the monastery of Valdemosa, on the island of Majorca, in 1839. They were first published by Ad. Catelin et Cie, Paris; by Breitkopf & Hartel, Leipzig; and by Wessel & Co., London. There are two "manuscripts."

1. The Autograph entirely in Chopin's own hand. This manuscript was meticulously prepared for publication. It includes careful indications of dynamics, phrasing and pedaling, together with marginal notes to the engraver. Although this manuscript is inscribed *"24 Preludes pour le pianoforte dediés a son ami J. C. Kessler par F. Chopin,"* it was from this manuscript that the first French edition (of Catelin et Cie) was made. The French edition was dedicated to Camille Pleyel. A facsimile edition of this manuscript is published by Polish Music Publications of Cracow (1951).

2. An authorized copy, probably by Julian Fontana. When Chopin finished the Autograph he wrote to Fontana, "I am sending you the Preludes. You and Wolff copy them. I think there are no errors." On this copy Fontana crossed out the dedication to J. C. Kessler and replaced it with *"Mr. Camille Pleyel par son ami."* At Chopin's instructions, however, he sent the original Autograph to Pleyel. The dedications were later properly credited by correspondence. This copy was used by the engraver of the first German edition (Breitkopf & Hartel) and the first English edition (Wessel & Co.).

The present edition is based on the Autograph. The copy, regardless of its excellence, can in no way serve to clarify the very legible and carefully prepared manuscript of Chopin, and contains a number of errors, as may be expected.

The two additional preludes included in this edition complete the known works of Chopin in this form. A prelude in C♯ minor, opus 45, composed in 1840, was dedicated to the Princess Elizabeth Czernicheff. A prelude in Ab major, without opus number, bears the dedication "A mon ami P. Wolff." The date of its composition is unknown. A facsimile of the autograph appeared in the Genevan periodical *Pages d'Art* in 1918.

THE PURPOSE OF THIS EDITION

It is the aim of the editor to convey as nearly as possible the intentions of the composer and to preserve all of the slurs, dynamic indications and pedal marks as well as the notation of the original manuscript. Since Chopin did not finger the Preludes, however, the fingering has been added by the editor in dark print.

This edition differs from the Autograph only in that the notes to be played by the right hand appear on the upper staff and the notes to be played by the left hand appear on the lower staff. In the few instances when the choice is optional there are footnotes to this effect. This type of scoring makes the music easier to read and eliminates much confusion, particularly with students in the early and intermediate grades.

Some editors have endeavored to "correct Chopin's mistakes" by changing measures that show slight variations upon repetition of similar themes. This is completely contrary to Chopin's style, which was generally to avoid exact repetitions. They have changed his harmonies, deleted his pedal indications completely, added cross-strokes to his appoggiaturas, and altered the phrasing which was so clearly indicated in the Autograph. We do not presume, as some editions do, to correct Chopin's harmony by the use of enharmonic writing. Chopin generally used the simplest notation, and we think it is presumptuous to correct his manuscript as if he were a student of harmony. Consequently, the notation found in this edition agrees precisely with the Autograph.

ORNAMENTATION

1. APPOGGIATURAS

Chopin used two types of single appoggiaturas:

a. The long appoggiatura, without a cross-stroke ♪ or ♩

b. The short appoggiatura, with a cross-stroke ♪̸

Each of these is played *ON THE BEAT*. The exact time consumed by the long appoggiatura is not always indicated by the type of small note used, as it was in the writing of C.P.E. Bach, but must be longer than the short appoggiatura, which is played very quickly.

Most modern editions of Chopin show all single appoggiaturas as short ones, with a cross-stroke. In the *PRELUDES*, there are many appoggiaturas without cross-strokes. We have left them as Chopin wrote them.

2. TURNS ∾

In Chopin's music the symbol for the turn is used as follows:

a. Directly over the note

In this case the turn begins on the note above the principal note.

Chopin's *Polonaise in B Major,* Posthumous (measure 13):

Written: Played:

b. After the note ♩ ∾

In this case the turn is played immediately after the principal note.

Chopin's *Prelude,* Op. 28, No. 4 (measure 16):

Written: Played:

OR:

3. TRILLS tr ∿∿∿

Karol Mikuli, who studied with Chopin for several years, quotes Chopin as saying that his trills generally begin on the upper note. This concept has also been confirmed by other students of Chopin, as well as by scholars who have studied the writings of Chopin's students.

When Chopin wanted a trill to begin on the principal note, he usually showed this by writing the appoggiatura sign at the same pitch as the principal note (ex. 1). That does not mean that this note should be repeated, but merely that the trill should begin on the principal note and not, as normally, on the upper note.

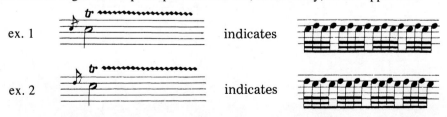

ex. 1   indicates

ex. 2   indicates

Chopin himself never did indicate the sign that shows the appoggiatura beginning on the upper note (ex. 2) because that practice was generally understood.

TRILLS (cont'd)

In the *PRELUDES*, most of the trills are preceded by a double appoggiatura, which becomes part of the trill and is therefore played on the beat. When the last note of the appoggiatura is the same as the principal note of the trill, the trill must begin on the upper auxiliary:

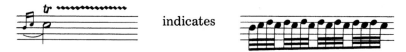

The number of repercussions in the trill depends, of course, on the tempo of the selection.

In many cases the trill is also followed by two small notes which form the suffix of the trill. These notes must be included as part of the complete ornament. Since they serve as the termination of the trill, they must not be played on the following count. Chopin has made this clear by placing such small notes before the bar line when this type of ornamentation occurs at the end of a measure.

Chopin's *Prelude*, Op. 28, No. 9 (measure 3):

Written: Played:

4. *ARPEGGIOS*

Arpeggios are often indicated by the symbol ⦙ or (beside the chord. The chords are broken, beginning with the lower note. If the symbol extends through both staffs, the chord is broken continuously from the lowest to the highest note. If each hand has a separate sign, one above the other, the two hands may begin simultaneously, or the right hand may begin immediately after the first note of the left hand is played. In such cases the arpeggios begin on the beat.

When only the right hand has an arpeggio, it generally begins on the beat. In some cases a left hand arpeggio may anticipate the beat, so the last note occurs on the beat coinciding with the corresponding right hand note.

Arpeggios are often written out in small notes. These are usually played on the following beat.

In the Library of the Paris Conservatoire, there is a copy of the first French Edition of Chopin's works, containing notations in Chopin's own hand for one of his pupils. In the *Nocturne*, Op. 37, No. 1 (measure 37), we find the following:

The dotted lines were written in by Chopin to show that the first note of each arpeggio is to be played *ON THE BEAT*.

5. GROUPS OF SMALL NOTES ♪ ♪♪ ♪♪♪ etc.

Groups of small notes are sometimes double or triple appoggiaturas, etc., sometimes turns or inverted turns, and sometimes the termination of trills.

When they are appoggiaturas, they are generally played on the beat. If they are turns, they are played before the beat, and if they are terminations of trills, they are played as part of the preceding ornament, as has already been noted.

PEDALING

The Pleyel piano used by Chopin to complete the *PRELUDES* was a small upright. It was not cross-strung, and lacked the resonance of the modern piano. Chopin preferred uprights to grands. This accounts for many of the indications for long sustained pedaling, which are often inappropriate on the modern piano.

Chopin was recognized in his own time for making great contributions to the art of pedaling, and his pedal markings are not to be ignored. He used the symbols *ped* ✿ to show the application and release of the pedal. These markings are not as precise as the 20th-century └────────────┘, and with them it is not as easy to show when a pedal is released and depressed again on the same note (└──────∧──────┘). It is for this reason that the present edition has adopted the more recently developed system.

It is true that Chopin's scores seldom show pedaling that is "overlapped," and he usually indicates └────────┘ └────────┘, which is known as "rhythmic pedaling," in which the pedal is released on one note and depressed on the following note. In some cases the more modern pedaling is preferred by many pianists. The two effects are different, however, and Chopin's indications deserve consideration. Occasionally, the sign indicating the release of the pedal was written above the sign indicating the depression of the pedal for the next group of notes. In other cases, the signs appear so close together, it seems that Chopin intended an overlapping pedal. In the cases where this occurs, the indication └─────∧─────┘ is used in this edition.

An examination of Chopin's pedal indications reveals that he sometimes omitted pedal marks in measures which were obviously pedaled the same as preceding ones. These omissions are especially frequent when an entire phrase occurring earlier in the composition is repeated. In this edition, we have supplemented the pedal markings in such cases, but we have indicated the editorial additions with the use of lighter print for entire pedal marks and dotted lines for releases within pedal marks too long to be effective on the modern piano.

It is important that the modern pianist observe the extent of a long group of notes that Chopin wished connected by means of the pedal, and through judicious application of modern pedaling techniques, he can retain much of the sound Chopin desired without blurring the total effect. This may be accomplished by the use of short "overlapping" pedaling and by half-pedaling (depressing the sustaining pedal only enough to leave the more resonant bass tones audible).

The student should not be puzzled by the use of staccato marks on notes that are sustained with the pedal. These marks serve to indicate the type of attack and release given to these notes by the hands and have nothing to do with staccato in the sense of shortening the note values.

CHOPIN AND THE CLEMENTI METHOD

Chopin used Muzio Clementi's popular method book, INTRODUCTION TO THE ART OF PLAYING ON THE PIANOFORTE, for his beginning students. He also used Clementi's GRADUS AD PARNASSUM. He taught works of Handel, Bach and Scarlatti. Chopin intended to write a method book of his own but left only a few preliminary notes. In these notes he emphasized the importance of playing with good fingering, of playing with the forearm and upper arm in addition to the wrist, hand and fingers. Like Bach and Clementi, he emphasized the importance of *LEGATO* playing and advised his students to listen to great singers and imitate their legato in cantilena playing. If Chopin taught the Clementi method verbatim, he taught that trills generally begin on the upper auxiliary and that all appoggiaturas are played on the beat.

TEMPO

Chopin did not indicate any metronome setting for the Preludes. A check of the metronome tempos of the available recordings of the Preludes shows a very wide divergence of opinions. Leonard Pennario, for example, plays the opening bars of Prelude No. 1 at a basic tempo c. ♩ = 138, while Brailowsky plays it at c. ♩ = 72, which, incidentally, is the tempo suggested in the old Kohler edition. Moravec, who plays Prelude No. 1 at c. ♩ = 60, varies the tempo in Prelude No. 21 as much as ♩ = 76 to ♩ = 92. A complete table of these metronome settings would serve only to provide statistics concerning the varying tempos used by the artists involved.

The question of tempo is not easily resolved and depends not only on factors of personal taste, but to some extent upon the individual instrument and the room or hall involved in the performance. The table below, from the edition of Louis Kohler, will provide one opinion for each of the Preludes. Others can be obtained by listening to the recommended recordings.

One cannot be certain that Chopin's playing was characterized by great freedom concerning fluctuations of tempo within a given selection. Chopin made no secret of his objection to exaggerated ritardandos and melodramatic display. He expressed admiration for the playing of J. B. Cramer, whom he said "plays beautifully and correctly and does not give way to passion like other young men." on more than one occasion he criticized Franz Liszt for taking excessive liberties with his music and the music of others, not only because of the notes he sometimes added or changed, but because of his "declamatory style."

METRONOME TEMPOS FROM THE KOHLER EDITION OF THE CHOPIN PRELUDES

No. 1. ♩ = 72 $\frac{2}{8}$	6. ♩ = 56 $\frac{3}{4}$	11. ♩. = 88 $\frac{6}{8}$	16. ♩ = 160 ¢	21. ♩ = 76 $\frac{3}{4}$
2. ♩ = 66 C	7. ♩ = 80 $\frac{3}{4}$	12. ♩. = 80 $\frac{3}{4}$	17. ♩. = 84 $\frac{6}{8}$	22. ♩. = 132 $\frac{6}{8}$
3. ♩ = 152 ¢	8. ♩ = 72 C	13. ♩. = 54 $\frac{6}{4}$	18. ♩ = 120 C	23. ♩ = 84 C
4. ♩ = 66 C	9. ♩ = 50 C	14. ♩ = 80 C	19. ♩ = 63 $\frac{3}{4}$	24. ♩. = 80 $\frac{6}{8}$
5. ♩. = 100 $\frac{3}{8}$	10. ♩ = 108 $\frac{3}{4}$	15. ♩ = 72 C	20. ♩ = 50 C	25. ♩ = 96 C

RUBATO

To Chopin's contemporaries, his rubato was the most unusual characteristic of his playing. Many found it difficult to understand such unprecedented freedom of rhythmic displacement. Perhaps they were unable to discern the underlying musical pulse, which, according to Chopin, Franz Liszt and many of Chopin's students, never varied. Chopin continually stressed the importance of maintaining regular meter in the accompaniment during rubato passages. His students testified that he demanded precise and perfectly measured rhythm. Franz Liszt described the Chopin rubato as never varying in the basic meter.

Detailed comments concerning Chopin's style may be found in Frederick Dorian's THE HISTORY OF MUSIC IN PERFORMANCE and Harold C. Schonberg's THE GREAT PIANISTS FROM MOZART TO THE PRESENT (see Recommended Reading, below).

RECOMMENDED RECORDINGS

The following recordings are recommended for listening and study.

CHOPIN: 24 PRELUDES, OP. 28, POLONAISE NO. 6, OP. 53, Geza Anda, Piano (Deutsche Grammophon 138 084)

CHOPIN: THE 24 PRELUDES, Alexander Brailowsky, Piano (Columbia MS 6119)

CHOPIN: TWENTY-FOUR PRELUDES, OP. 28, FANTASY IN F MINOR, OP. 49, BERCEUSE, OP. 57, Jeanne-Marie Darré, Piano (Vanguard VSD 71151)

CHOPIN: PRELUDES, OPUS 28, Ivan Moravec, Piano (Connoisseur Society CS1366)

FREDERIC CHOPIN: TWENTY-FOUR PRELUDES, OP. 28, Leonard Pennario, Piano (Capitol SP 8561)

CHOPIN PRELUDES, OP. 28, Artur Rubinstein, Piano (RCA Victor LM-1163)

RECOMMENDED READING

Dart, Thurston. THE INTERPRETATION OF MUSIC, Harper & Row, New York, 1963.

Dorian, Frederick. THE HISTORY OF MUSIC IN PERFORMANCE, W.W. Norton & Co., New York, 1942.

Eigeldinger, Jean-Jacques. CHOPIN, PIANIST AND TEACHER AS SEEN BY HIS PUPILS, Cambridge University Press, Cambridge, 1986.

Ferrá, Bartolomé. CHOPIN AND GEORGE SAND IN MAJORCA, Francisco Soler, Palma, 1936.

Huneker, James Gibbons. CHOPIN, THE MAN AND HIS MUSIC, C. Scribner & Sons, New York, 1901.

Schonberg, Harold C. THE GREAT PIANISTS FROM MOZART TO THE PRESENT, Simon and Schuster, New York, 1963.

Walker, Alan. CHOPIN: PROFILES OF THE MAN AND THE MUSICIAN, Barrie and Rockliff, London, 1966.

Weinstock, Herbert. CHOPIN: THE MAN AND HIS MUSIC, Alfred A. Knopf, New York, 1949.

Wierzynski, Casimir. THE LIFE AND DEATH OF CHOPIN, Simon and Schuster, New York, 1949.

ACKNOWLEDGEMENTS

I would like to express my thanks to Morton Manus and Arnold Rosen for their assistance in obtaining the microfilms of the original manuscripts and other important research materials; to Irving Chasnov for his valued suggestions and assistance in the preparation of the footnotes; to Judith Simon Linder for her alert and intelligent help with the arduous research necessary for the realization of this edition.

24 Preludes pour le pianoforte dediés a son ami J. C. Kessler par F. Chopin

Prelude in C Major

Agitato

Op. 28, No. 1

(a) Although the notation of the lowest treble voice is rhythmically inexact, the meaning is clear. It is given here as it appears in Chopin's manuscript except that all notes played by the right hand appear on the upper staff.

(b) Most editions show the pedal sustained for the full measure, for each of the first 32 measures. In the Autograph, the pedal indications differ from measure to measure, as we show them. In the 23rd measure, Chopin wrote one of the pedal releases just after the last note of the measure, then scratched it out and rewrote it under the next-to-last note. This seems to be evidence that all the pedal marks were carefully placed. We leave the decision to the individual.

ⓒ The quintuplets in measures 18, 19, 20, 23, 25 and 26 are clearly indicated in the Autograph. It is difficult to understand why some editors have altered these measures to conform to the rhythm of measures 1 through 17.

Prelude in A Minor

Op. 28, No. 2

(a) The two-part writing used in the first two measures emphasizes the importance of the upper voice of the accompaniment. It is possible that Chopin intended the notes with stems up to be played with the right hand, as he often did when he used two-part writing in similar instances in other compositions.

(b) In the Autograph, each of the appoggiaturas in this selection is written without a cross-stroke.

(c) This is the only pedal indication in this Prelude, in the Autograph.

Prelude in G Major

Op. 28, No. 3

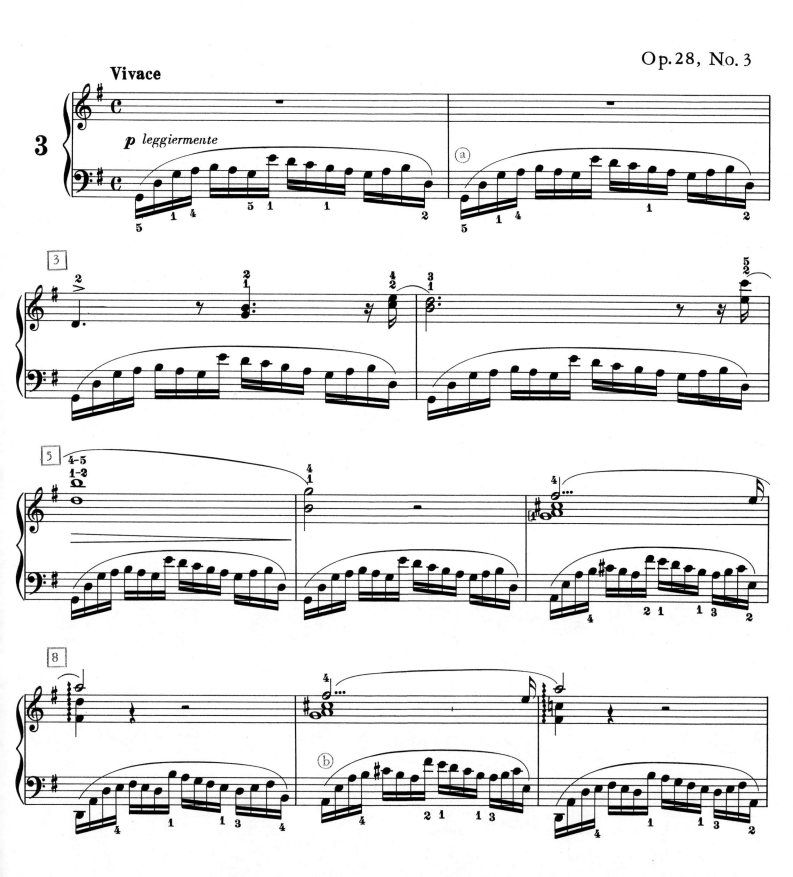

(a) In the Autograph, the slurs overlap in this and similar instances. This was in keeping with Chopin's usual style of writing slurs, but in this case, one may be sure that no break between slurs is intended.

(b) The crescendo found here in most recent editions is missing from the Autograph as well as from the first French and German editions.

16

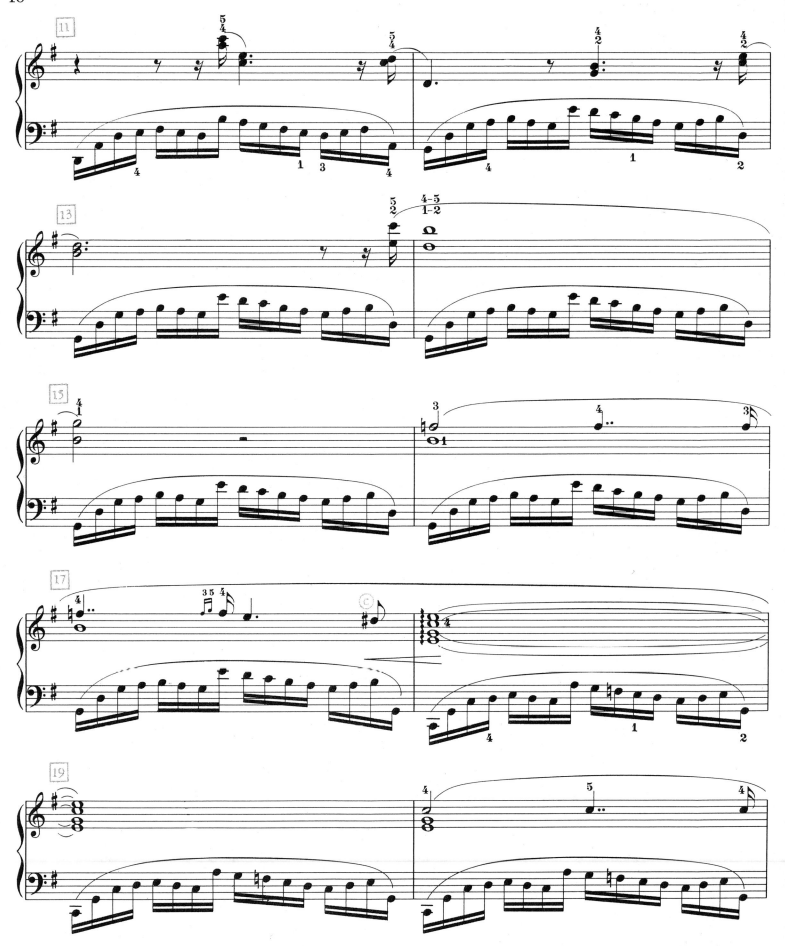

© In almost all recent editions, the D♯ is a sixteenth note, and the E before it is double-dotted. In the Autograph and in the first French edition, it appears as an eighth note. The cadence, the crescendo, and the arpeggiated chord following this note, set it apart from other notes and this is not, as some suggest, "obviously an oversight."

(d) The E and G are not tied to the previous measure, as shown in the Mikuli and Joseffy editions.

(e) Because of the left hand part, the right hand is usually played

Prelude in E Minor

Op. 28, No.4

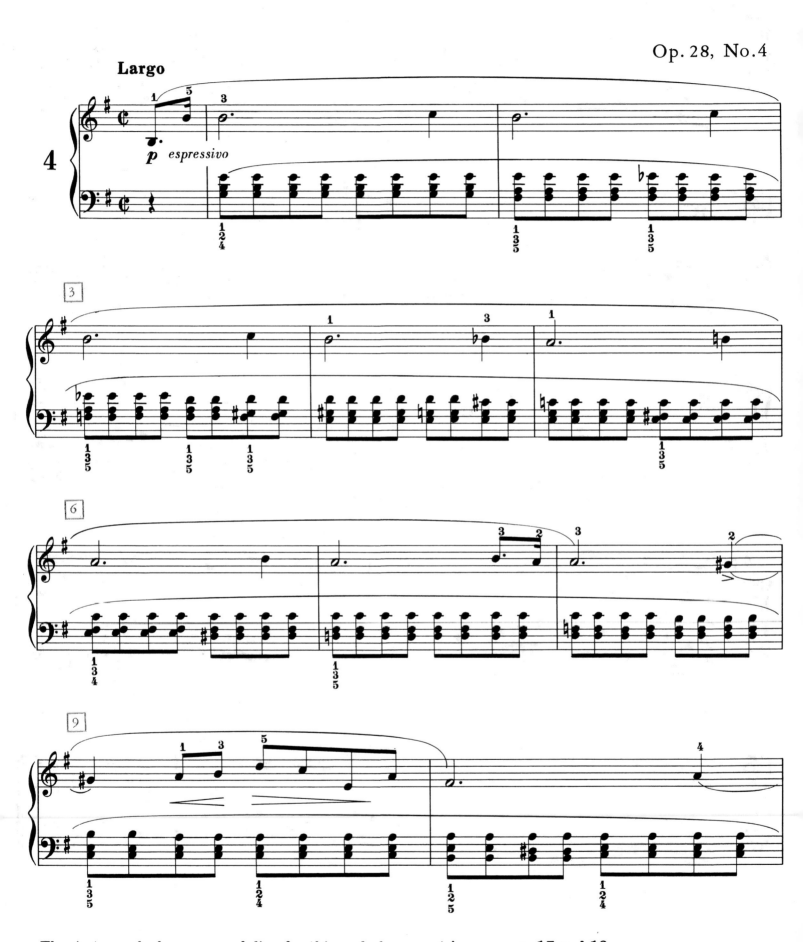

The Autograph shows no pedaling for this prelude, except in measures 17 and 18.

19

ⓐ The appoggiatura has no cross-stroke.

ⓑ Many editions show a dynamic indication "p" and a diminuendo in the previous measure. The Autograph has a crescendo in the 12th measure, as shown.

Prelude in D Major

Op. 28, No. 5

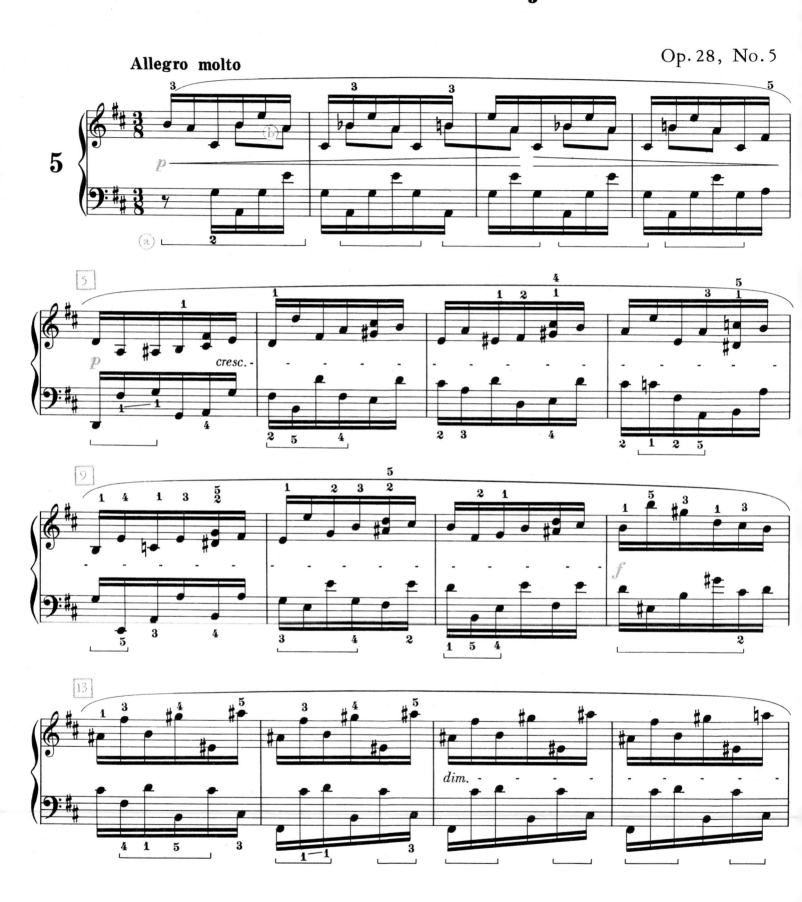

(a) The pedaling given here is exactly as in the Autograph.

(b) The eighth note is held into the following measure.   The function of the eighth notes is made clear in the 2nd and 3rd measures.   Some editors change this note to a sixteenth note in the inner voice as well as the upper voice. Chopin's notation may be unconventional but it is also ingenious.

21

© No pedaling appears in the Autograph in measures 21 through 28.

ⓓ The left hand chord should sound with the right hand chord. In this case, the small note may anticipate the beat.

Prelude in B Minor

Op.28, No.6

Prelude in A Major

Op. 28, No. 7

Prelude in F♯ Minor

Op. 28, No. 8

Molto agitato

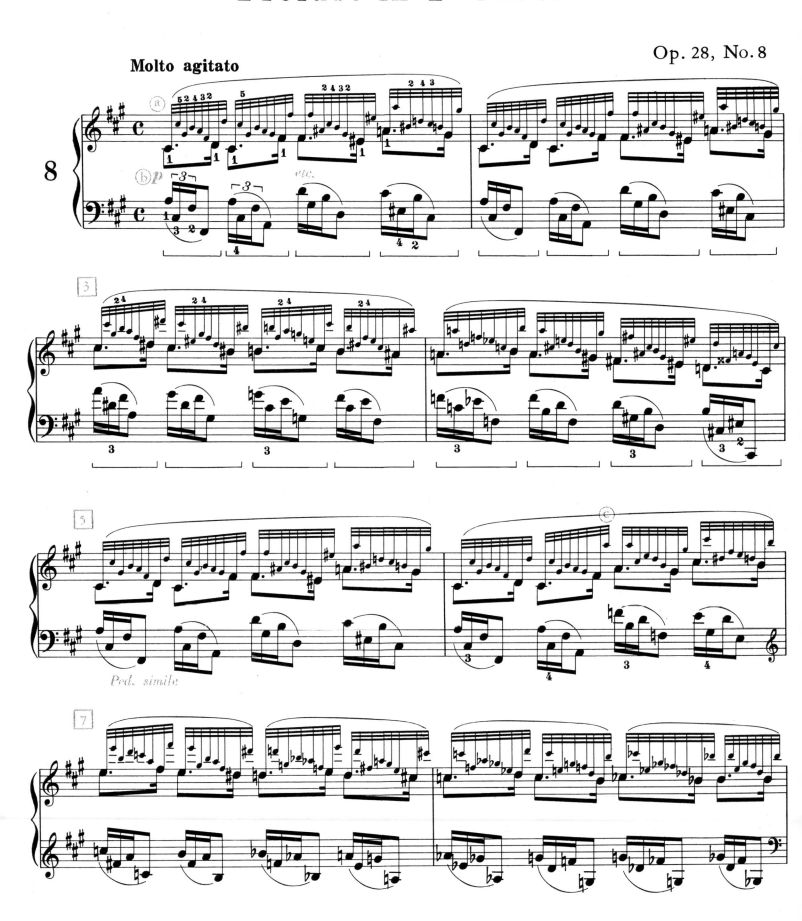

ⓐ The slurs agree with those of the Autograph.

ⓑ Most editions abound in dynamic signs, crescendos and diminuendos not indicated by Chopin himself. The "p" at measure 19 has influenced the editor to select this volume, rather than "mf" to begin this prelude.

ⓒ Some editions have F♯. The A appears in the Autograph and all early editions.

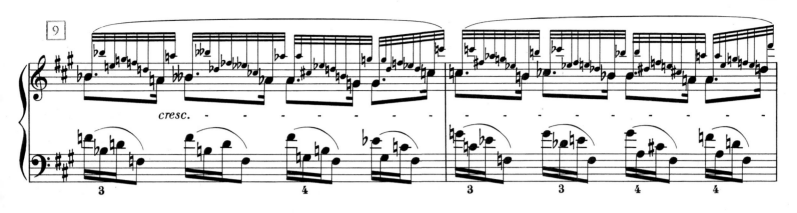

26

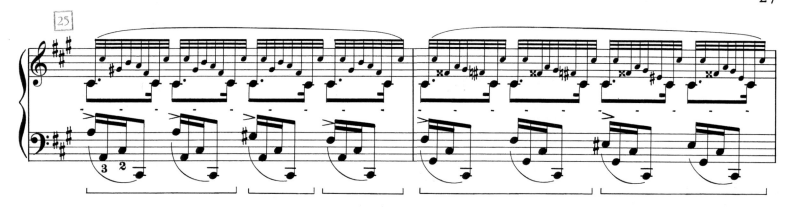

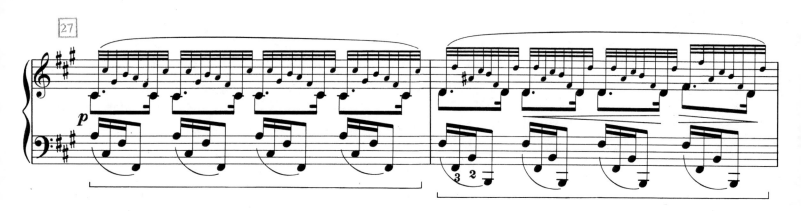

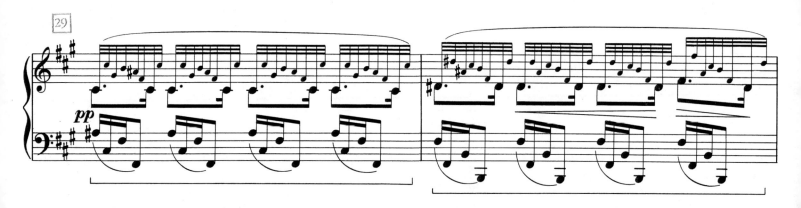

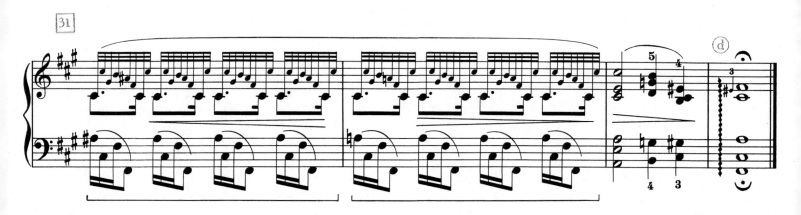

(d) The appoggiatura appears as a small quarter note. It can be interpreted only as a LONG APPOGGIATURA. The measure is played thus:

Prelude in E Major

Op. 28, No. 9

The notation used here agrees with that of the first editions. In the Autograph, all of the sixteenth notes are written directly over the last note of the triplet group. Most of the thirty-second notes were written in similar fashion and later shifted, with the original notes scratched out. This seems to indicate the dotted notes should be observed at their proper values.

ⓐ The small notes preceding the trill must be considered as part of the ornament and played ON THE BEAT (see page 7). The small notes following the trill form the suffix of the trill and are played AHEAD of the following beat. The trills may be played with more repercussions.

(b) The Autograph and the French edition have B♭, contrary to some editions which have B♮ .

(c) The Autograph and the original editions agree on the notation here. Joseffy and Mikuli show the second eighth note as it would normally occur, just before the last double note of the triplet group.

(d) This is the exact location of the ⟩ in the Autograph. The word "decresc." is also written here, superimposed on the converging lines.

Prelude in C♯ Minor

Allegro molto

(a) Some players will prefer to pedal ⌐⌐⌐ etc. The type of pedaling indicated by Chopin is known as "rhythmic pedaling" and produces a slightly different effect.

(b) The sixteenth rests appearing here in some editions, making the notation of the right hand rhythm agree exactly with the left hand, do not appear in the Autograph in this and similar measures, except in the very last measure of the selection.

(c) The small notes are played as part of the trill, starting on the beat. See footnote (a) of Prelude No.9 and the discussion of trills on pages 7 and 8. The trill may have more repercussions.

(d) The slur from B♯ appears in the Autograph but was crossed out by Chopin
and replaced by the longer slur from the A in the previous measure:

Prelude in B Major

Op. 28, No. 11

(a) Some pianists may prefer to substitute ⎣ʌ⎣ʌ⎣ etc. for the "rhythmic pedaling" indicated by Chopin.

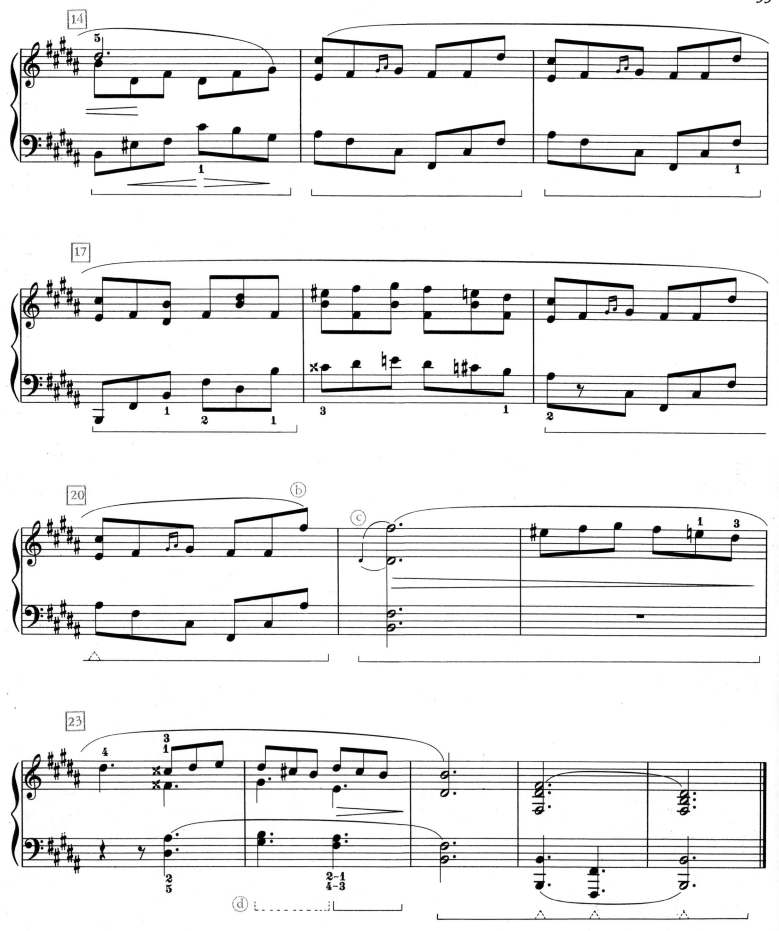

ⓑ The Mikuli edition has D♯ instead of F♯. The Autograph has F♯.

ⓒ The Autograph shows the appoggiatura as a small quarter note without a flag or cross-stroke. It should be played ON THE BEAT.

ⓓ The pedal notation here is indefinite in the Autograph.

Prelude in G♯ Minor

Op. 28, No. 12

(a) The pedal marks are omitted here in the Autograph. The marks suggested are taken from measures 49 and 50, in which the notes are identical to measures 9 and 10.

ⓑ In the Autograph and the French edition, the B's are not tied, as they are in many modern editions.

ⓒ The C♮ in the Mikuli, Joseffy and other editions is incorrect. The Autograph has C♯, as do the first French and German editions.

ⓓ The A in the upper voice is a quarter note in the Autograph and first editions. Most modern editions show it as a dotted half note, as in measure 25.

ⓔ The A♮'s are not tied as in most editions.

ⓕ The D's are natural in the Autograph and first editions. Most modern edition's have D♯.

(g) The F♯ in parentheses is omitted in the Autograph and first editions.

Prelude in F♯ Major

Op. 28, No. 13

(a) The Autograph has the time signature crossed out and replaced with "$\frac{3}{2}$".

(b) The slur ends here, contrary to many editions.

(c) The whole note is very clear in the Autograph. Most editions show a dotted half note.

(d) The rest is omitted from most editions but is very clear in the Autograph.

(e) The appoggiatura is written as a small quarter note without a cross-stroke. It is certainly intended as a long appoggiatura. The nearly vertical slur indicates the arpeggio (see page 8).

39

In some editions, an eighth rest appears in place of the first E♯ in this measure. The Autograph and first edition clearly show E♯ here.

(g) The three-note chord with downstems is not arpeggiated. The dotted whole note is added quickly and sustained with the pedal. The vertical slur (, shown here exactly as in the Autograph, serves to indicate the point at which the chord must be broken and makes the intentions of the composer very clear.

Prelude in E♭ Minor

Op. 28, No. 14

(a) In a copy of the first French edition, belonging to one of his pupils, Chopin crossed out the word "Allegro" and wrote above it "Largo", in big letters.

(b) Many editions have a time signature of **C**, but the Autograph has **¢**.

(c) The natural sign is missing from the Autograph.

43

ⓓ In the Autograph, no accidental appears before this note.

Prelude in D♭ Major

Op. 28, No. 15

(a) Several of the pedal indications in the Autograph have the symbol for the release of one pedal almost directly above the indication for the application of the following pedal. We have interpreted this to indicate "overlapping" of pedals. We have shown as clearly as possible the pedaling indicated by Chopin, and we must leave the interpretation and application of these indications to the individual.

(b) Some editors have added quarter-note stems to this and many other eighth notes. Only those shown in the Autograph are included here.

(c) Mikuli and Joseffy have added dots to the half notes. The Autograph and first French and German editions show no dots after these notes in this and similar measures.

(d) Many editions show the upper note of the left hand (G♭) as a dotted eighth note. The Autograph and first French and German editions show this and similar measures as we have presented them.

(e) Because the grace note is an anticipation, it is played before the beat.

(f) No dots appear after the half notes in the Autograph and first French and German editions.

(g) The slur is not broken here, as some editions show.

(h) In the Autograph, the slur ends here, contrary to most editions.

(i) The slur begins on the second note of the measure.

(j) Many editions show a diminuendo. It does not appear in the Autograph.

(k) The grace note has no cross-stroke.

① This pedal mark should probably agree with measure 1.

ⓜ This pedal mark has no release indicated in the Autograph.

Prelude in B♭ Minor

Op. 28, No. 16

(a) The first French edition has a time signature of **C**. The Autograph and first German edition have **¢**.

(b) The single pedal for the entire measure, though rarely found in modern editions, agrees with the Autograph and first French and German editions.

(c) The single pedal lasting for three measures and the very long pedal marks that follow are according to the original version. The dotted wedges are added by the editor, because such pedaling is preferred by most performers, due to the resonance of the modern piano. The long pedals deserve a trial, however, and the effect may be more nearly in accordance with Chopin's intentions.

(d) The flat does not appear in the Autograph. It is possibly an oversight, since this corresponds to measure 23. Some editions change measure 23 to correspond to measure 7, adding a ♮ sign before the A.

50

(f) The slur under the lower staff is not in the Autograph but is undoubtedly intended. The slur over the upper staff was probably considered sufficient to convey the proper manner of execution.

Prelude in A♭ Major

Op. 28, No. 17

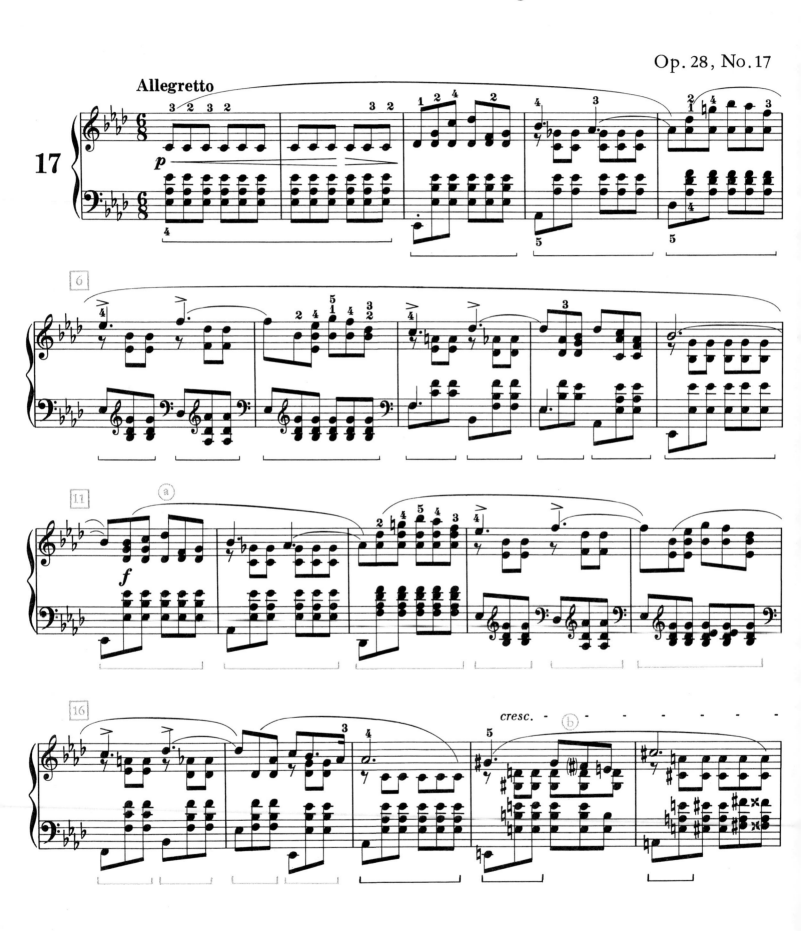

(a) Some editions add a G between the two D♭'s. It does not appear in the Autograph.

(b) The accidental sign in parentheses in this and other measures of this Prelude are missing from the Autograph (measures 26, 33, 44, 45 and 48).

(c) The arpeggio is played on the 2nd count, followed by the appoggiatura. One correct way of performing this is as follows:

(d) In some recent editions the B♮ is tied to the first note of the next measure. It is not tied in the Autograph or the first French and German editions.

(e) Some editions show an arpeggio sign similar to the one in measure 43. The Autograph shows a slur, written in the manner reproduced in this edition, which probably did indicate an arpeggio. If an arpeggio is used, it should be played in the same manner as the one in measure 43. See the discussion on page 8.

(f) In some editions, the C♯ is tied to the first note of the following measure. It is not tied in the original version.

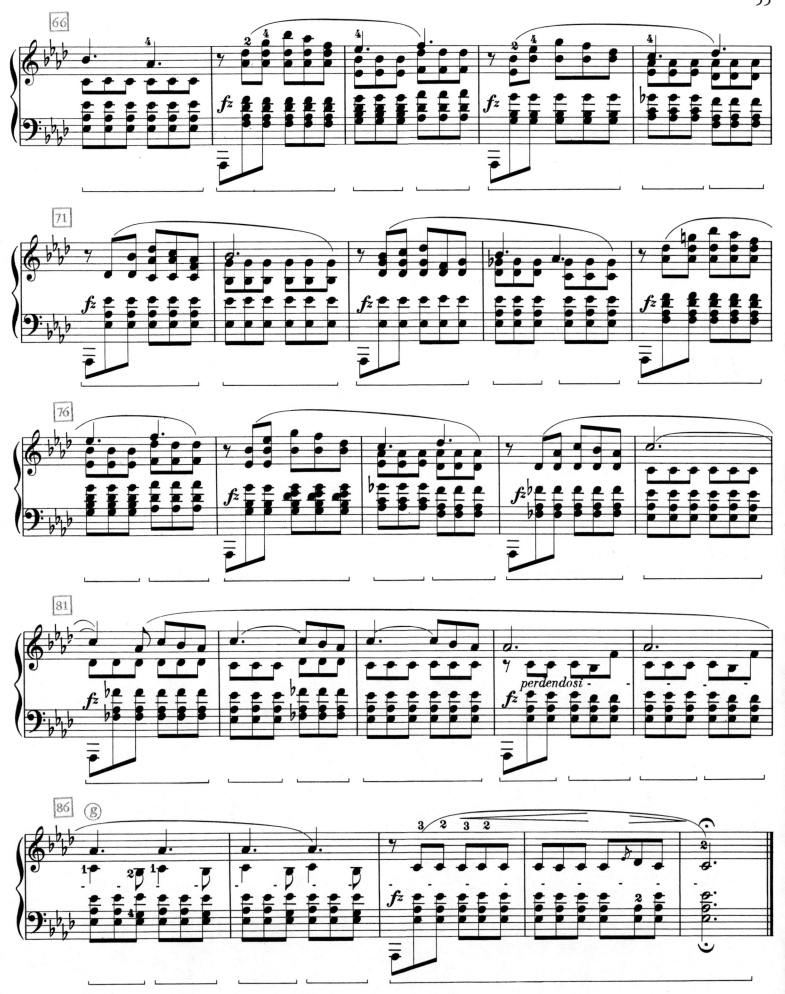

g In the Autograph and the first French and German editions, this and the following three A♭'s appear as quarter notes without rests. The dots are added in the first English edition, as well as the Mikuli and other editions. Joseffy adds eighth rests.

Prelude in F Minor

Op. 28, No. 18

(a) The Autograph and first German edition have ₵. The first French edition has C.

(b) The flat is not restored to the E in the Autograph or in the first French and German editions. The first English edition shows E♭, as do the Mikuli and Joseffy editions.

© This pedaling differs from most recent editions but is very clearly indicated in the Autograph.

Prelude in E♭ Major

Op. 28 , No. 19

(a) Joseffy adds quarter-note stems to the first note of each triplet. This was not done by Chopin.

(b) The third note of the first triplet is shown in some recent editions as G, agreeing with measure 9. The Autograph and the first French and German editions have E, as do Mikuli and Joseffy.

(c) Chopin omits the pedaling here for three measures, which are obviously pedaled the same as the first three measures.

(d) See (b) on the previous page. The same discrepancies occur here in various editions due to the fact that Chopin did not re-write these measures, but only indicated that measures 1 through 10 were to be inserted at this point.

60

(e) Some recent editions have "improved" Chopin's original version by changing the G in the left hand to a B. The Autograph and first editions show G very clearly.

(f) The continuous decrescendo beginning here, clearly indicated in the Autograph, has been ignored by the Mikuli, Joseffy and other editions.

(g) The quarter note stems added to the last note of the triplet here and to the last two triplets of the next measure emphasize the chromatic progression. They appear in the Autograph but are omitted in most editions.

(h) The final pedal indication is very clear in the Autograph. Most editors find this incredible, it seems, since they terminate the pedal on the first note of the 69th measure.

Prelude in C Minor

Op. 28, No. 20

(a) According to the editors of the Oxford edition, Chopin is supposed to have added a flat sign before the E in a copy belonging to one of his pupils. It does not appear in the Autograph or the original editions.

(b) A TEMPO is inferred by Chopin in his manner of writing these measures, which was simply to indicate that measures 5 through 8 are repeated.

(c) This is the only pedal indication in the Autograph.

Prelude in B♭ Major

Op. 28, No. 21

(a) The appoggiatura appears in the Autograph as a small quarter note. It must be interpreted as a long appoggiatura.

(b) The dot was removed (crossed out) from the G in this measure by Chopin. The quarter rest is added by the editor.

(c) In the Autograph, the E♭ is written on the treble staff, exactly as shown here. This indicated that the E♭ is to be played by the right hand, to facilitate execution. The copyist mistakenly took this as a melody note and gave it the value of a quarter note. This error was reproduced in the first editions.

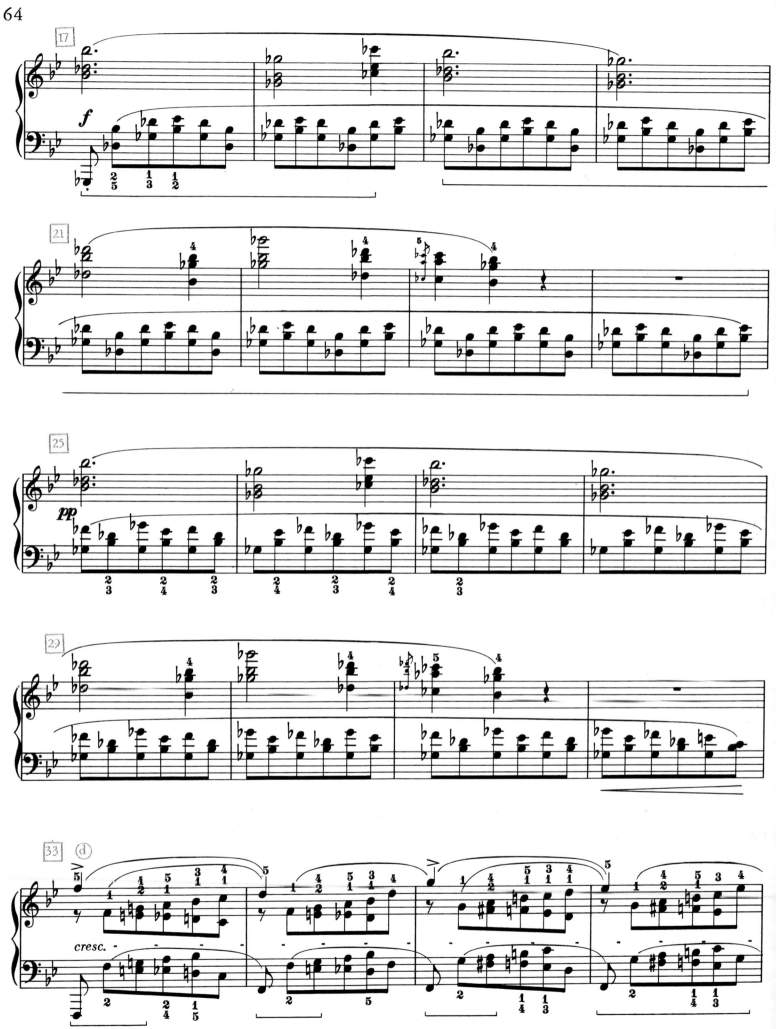

(d) The slurs in the present edition are taken from the Autograph.

(e) In the Autograph, the G♭ and E♭ are joined by a quarter note stem, as shown. In most editions, only the E♭ has the quarter note stem.

(f) The dots after the G's are omitted in the Autograph and the first editions.

(g) This entire measure is missing in many editions. It was omitted from the first German edition due to a copyist's error. Other editions, including Mikuli, Joseffy and Peters, have failed to correct the mistake. It appears clearly in the Autograph and first French edition.

Prelude in G Minor

Molto agitato

Op. 28, No. 22

(a) In the Autograph, the eighth note flag is missing. The chord cannot have the value of a quarter note, since all the rests shown above also appear in the Autograph. Some editions leave the chord as a quarter note, deleting the following eighth rest.

(b) The small decrescendo signs ⟩ are interpreted by some editors as accent marks.

Prelude in F Major

Op. 28, No. 23

(a) The more modern pedaling └───⌃─── etc. may be preferred by some pianists. The pedaling shown above agrees with the Autograph.

(b) See the discussion of trills on pages 7 and 8. The trills in measures 6, 10 and 18 are realized in a similar manner. The number of repercussions depends upon the tempo.

Prelude in D Minor

Op. 28, No. 24

(a) The continuous pedal from measures 1 through 4 is in accordance with the Autograph.

(b) The Autograph shows a continuous pedal from measure 6 until the beginning of the trill in measure 10. The dotted wedges are editorial suggestions. Half-pedaling may be effective in this and other measures in which the pedaling seems excessively sustained for the resonance of the modern piano.

(c) See the discussion of the trill on pages 7 and 8. The trill in measure 28 should be played in the same manner.

(d) The trill may possibly begin on the upper note. The trills in measures 16, 30 and 34 must be played in the same manner as this trill.

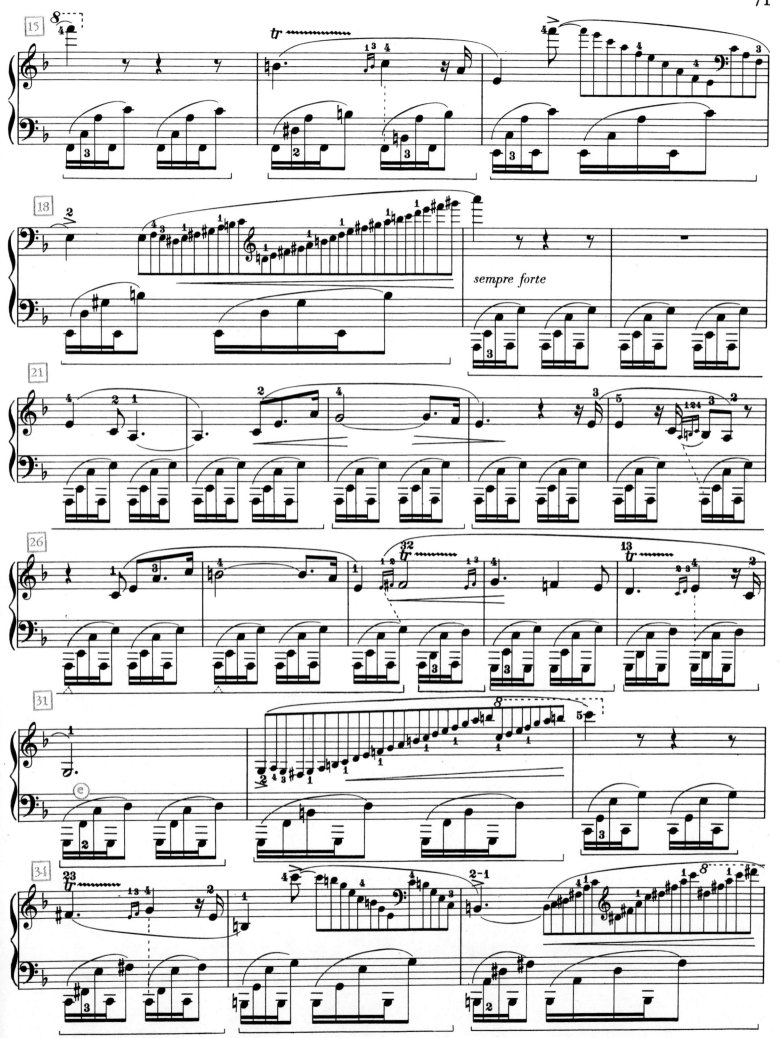

(e) The first German edition has D instead of F here and in the following group of notes.   The Autograph and the first French edition have F, as shown.

(f) The "sempre ff" and diminuendo occurring simultaneously in most editions is confusing only because other editions show the diminuendo extending over to include the descending arpeggio. The Autograph clearly shows that diminuendo includes only the first five notes of the left hand. The descending right hand arpeggio begins after the diminuendo, and the "sempre ff" obviously applies to the arpeggio, which ends on the accented D in the following measure.

A Mademoiselle la Princess Elizabeth Czernicheff

Prelude in C# Minor

Op. 45

(a) Some recent editions have F♯, rather than A, which appears in the first French and German editions.

A mon ami P. Wolff

Prelude in A♭ Major

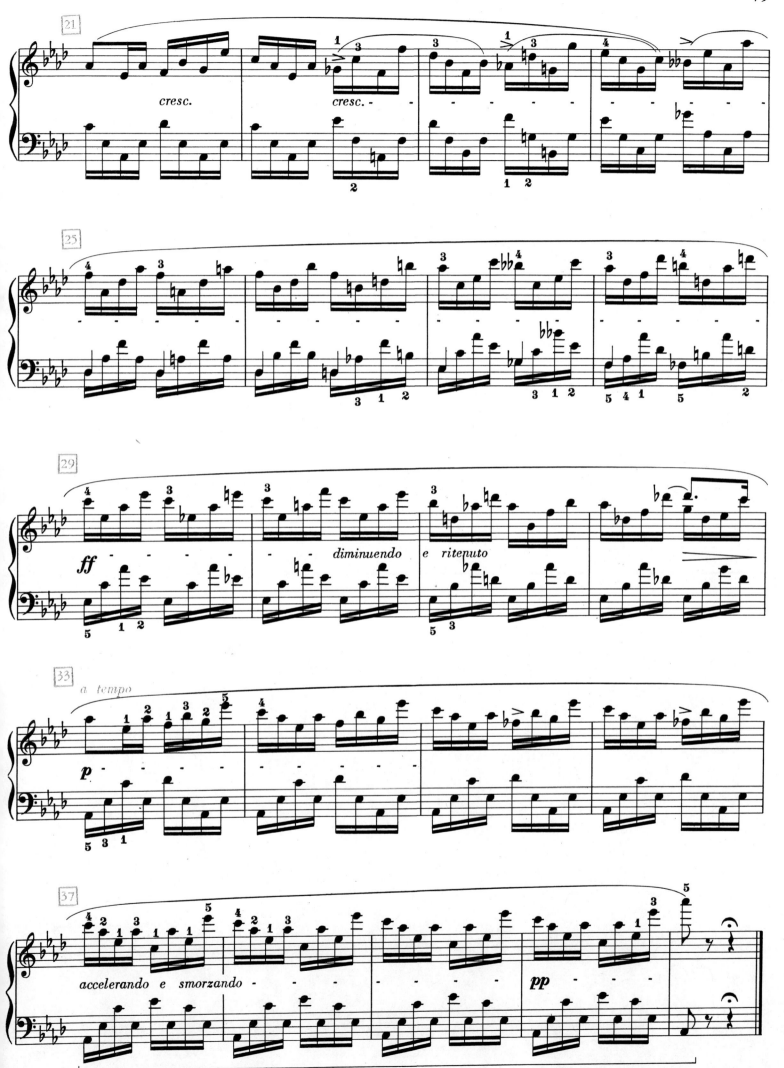